Don't Spill The Seed

Printed in the United States of America

First Printing, 2024

ISBN 978-1-954829-17-6

First Edition

Dear Seed Growers!

Welcome to Don't Spill the Seed! What an awesome title, right?! The title means so many things. This course is more than just about building a successful short-term rental or Airbnb business. It's about cultivating character and sustainable traits that will keep you in that place of success. A strong character will sustain you through the test of time. We all sow seeds, whether good or bad, and you plant seeds every day with your words. This course will teach you how to grow and sow the types of seeds you want. Not only will you learn how to build a successful business, but also how to guide others to do the same.

We are super excited that you embarked on this journey with us! Now buckle up and let's enjoy the ride!

Management

Table of Contents

Steps to a successful short-term rental business!

Mission

Our mission is to help build a million business owners using sustainable principles!

Principles

What kind of principles are you operating your business on? What core values are important for your business?

So often people start businesses, but they don't stop to define the core values or principles they want to operate within. Principles are a critical part of the success of your business. When you establish principles or core values, you can train your staff on what your beliefs are and what you will or will not tolerate.

Core Values (sample of what our company is built on)

- Integrity
- Trust
- Hard Work
- Punctuality
- Respect
- Excellence

- Love is in everything that we do
- Communication
- Support
- Creating a safe space/environment
- Community
- Innovation

Core values are the fundamental beliefs and guiding principles that dictate behavior and action within an individual or an organization. They serve as a foundation for decision-making and help shape the culture and identity. Outline what your core values mean to you and your company. How will you use or implement these items in your business.

Steps to a Successful Short-term Rental business

Forming a Business:

1. Check the name on your local state government website.
   a. For example: For Ohio you would go to: Homepage - Ohio Secretary of State (ohiosos.gov)
2. Decide whether to operate as a sole proprietorship, partnership, corporation, or LLC (Limited Liability Company). Consider factors such as liability, taxation, and administrative requirements when choosing your structure. If the name is not taken, complete the registration form to form your business. (Please consult with legal counsel or the government at the state or federal level to determine what type of business you should form. We cannot give you legal advice in this area).
3. Apply for an EIN from the Internal Revenue Service (IRS) if you plan to hire employees or operate as a corporation or partnership. (Apply for an Employer Identification Number (EIN) online | Internal Revenue Service (irs.gov).
4. Obtain the necessary licenses and permits required for your industry and location. Consult with your local state government or attorney to ensure you have the proper licenses and permits.
5. Separate your personal and business finances by opening a dedicated business bank account.
6. Consider getting a business credit card to manage business expenses and build credit.

Notes:

_____

_____

_____

_____

_____

_____

_____

_____

_____

_____

_____

_____

_____

_____

_____

_____

_____

_____

_____

_____

_____

_____

_____

_____

_____

_____

_____

Setting Goals

Short Term Goals

1. How many properties do you want to own or acquire in the next six months?

   _____

   _____

   _____

2. How much money would you like to see your company gross in the next 6 months to a year?

   _____

3. What are the key milestones that you need to hit in order to achieve your goals listed above?

   _____

   _____

   _____

   _____

4. What immediate actions can you take to move closer to these goals each day?

   _____

   _____

   _____

   _____

5. What skills or knowledge do you need to develop or improve to achieve these goals?

   _____

   _____

_____

_____

6. Who can you collaborate with or seek support from to achieve my goals?

_____

_____

_____

7. How will you stay motivated and focused on your goal? What is your why?

_____

_____

_____

_____

_____

Long-Term Goals

1. Where do you see your business in 1 year (use as much detail as possible)?

_____

_____

_____

_____

_____

_____

2. How many properties would you like to own or acquire in the next year (use as much detail as possible)?

_____

_____

_____

_____

_____

3. What are your core values and how can they guide your long-term goals?

_____

_____

_____

_____

_____

4. What legacy do you want to leave behind?

_____

_____

_____

_____

5. What significant accomplishments do you want to achieve in my
   business?

_____

_____

_____

_____

6. What kind of lifestyle do you aspire to have in the future?

_____

_____

_____

_____

7. What kind of impact do you want to make in your community or
   industry?

_____

_____

_____

_____

_____

Quotes from Famous People

"Don't aspire to make a living, aspire to make a difference." Denzel Washington

"I am not looking back for who left. I am looking forward for WHO's next!" Tiana Jones

"Persist, Pivot or Concede. It's up to us, our choice every time." Matthew McConaughey

"My career is the sum of the decisions I have made." Priyanka Chopra

"Other people's opinion of you does not have to become your reality." Les Brown

"It's not over until I win!" Les Brown

"In the middle of difficulty lies opportunity." Albert Einstein

"You never fail until you stop trying." Albert Einstein

"Turn your wounds into wisdom." Oprah Winfrey

"Doing the best at this moment, puts you in best place for the next moment." Oprah Winfrey

"It doesn't matter if a million people tell you what you can't do, or if ten million tell you no. If you get one yes from God, that's all you need." Tyler Perry

Success is not how high you have climbed, but how you make a positive difference to the world." Roy T. Bennett

"Nothing is impossible, the word itself says, I'm possible!" Audrey Hepburn

 "Success is liking yourself, liking what you do and liking how you do it." Maya Angelou

State/City Regulations for Short-term Rentals

Many cities around the world have implemented regulations or outright bans on Airbnb and other short-term rental platforms due to concerns about housing affordability, neighborhood disruption, and tax compliance. Here are some notable cities with strict regulations or bans:

- **New York City, USA**: Short-term rentals of less than 30 days are generally illegal if the host is not present, especially in multi-unit buildings.
- **San Francisco, USA**: Hosts are required to register with the city, and there are limits on the number of days a property can be rented out if the host is not present.
- **Los Angeles, USA**: Hosts must register and cannot rent out properties for more than 120 days per year without additional permits.
- **Las Vegas, USA**: Short-term rentals are heavily regulated, with strict licensing requirements and zoning restrictions.
- **Miami, USA**: Regulations vary by neighborhood, with many areas prohibiting short-term rentals altogether.
- **Santa Monica, USA**: Hosts must be present during the stay, and properties must be registered with the city.
- **Paris, France**: Short-term rentals are limited to 120 days per year, and hosts must register with the city.
- **Berlin, Germany**: Short-term rentals are heavily restricted, and hosts must obtain a permit from the city.
- **Barcelona, Spain**: Strict licensing requirements are in place, and new licenses are difficult to obtain.
- **Amsterdam, Netherlands**: Short-term rentals are limited to 30 days per year, and hosts must register with the city.
- **Tokyo, Japan**: Short-term rentals are limited to 180 days per year, and hosts must comply with strict regulations.

- **Vancouver, Canada**: Short-term rentals are only allowed in primary residences, and hosts must obtain a business license.

This does not include all cities and states but it outlines some of the most notable ones. Please be sure to check your local state regulations to ensure you are in compliance with all short-term rental laws.

Finding Properties

Side Note: you do not have to own a home to do short-term rentals – more information will be provided during the online course.

Finding properties is one of the most important things you will do when looking for short-term or rental properties in general. It's important to think outside of the box. So many people are focused on the attractions around when looking for Airbnb's or short-term rentals. That is only half of it. When I look for properties, I think of "what families may want" not the average tourists. Families are looking for properties that feel like home or a home away from home. They want somewhere they can enjoy each other. I am saying that to say, looking for major cities is not always the key. Look for properties where you would want to live. So many people ask me time and time again, why I have properties in certain locations but nothing close to the city. My answer every time is that I know my audience and my target market. I am not looking for the partiers or just to rent out my properties for "a good time." I want people to leave feeling like they had an experience, or they felt at home. Try to find properties that are close to the highway for easy access. That way if they want to go into the city or visit any other surrounding cities, they have easy access to a highway.

Apartments (Advantages vs. Disadvantages)

The decision between choosing an apartment versus a house often involves weighing various factors such as lifestyle preferences, financial considerations, and long-term goals. Here are some key points to consider:

Apartments

Advantages:

- **Lower Maintenance**: Apartments typically require less maintenance and upkeep, as property management usually handles repairs and maintenance tasks.

- **Amenities**: Many apartment complexes offer amenities such as pools, gyms, and common areas, which can be costly to install and maintain in a house.

- **Location**: Apartments are often located in urban areas with easy access to public transportation, entertainment, and job opportunities.

- **Cost**: Generally, the upfront cost of renting an apartment is lower compared to buying a house. This includes lower down payments and monthly expenses.

Disadvantages:

- **Space**: Apartments usually offer less living space compared to houses, which can be a limitation for families or individuals who need more room.

- **Equity**: Renting an apartment does not build equity, as the property does not belong to the renter.

- **Privacy and Control**: Apartment living can offer less privacy and control over the living environment, including noise from neighbors and restrictions on renovations.

Houses

Advantages:

- **Equity Building**: Owning a home allows you to build equity over time, which can be a significant financial advantage.

- **Space**: Houses generally offer more living space, including yards and additional rooms, which can be important for families.

- **Customization**: Homeowners have more freedom to renovate and customize their living space according to their preferences.

Disadvantages:

- **Maintenance and Costs**: Owning a house involves ongoing maintenance and repairs, which can be time-consuming and expensive.

- **Higher Upfront Costs**: The initial costs of buying a house, including down payments, closing costs, and moving expenses, are typically higher than renting an apartment.

- **Location**: Houses are often located in suburban or rural areas, which may require longer commutes and less access to urban amenities.

Financial Considerations

When it comes to financial gains, owning a home can potentially be more lucrative in the long run due to the accumulation of equity and potential property value appreciation. However, it's also important to consider market conditions, interest rates, and personal financial situations. Renting an apartment may be more cost-effective and flexible in the short term, especially for those who move frequently or are not ready for the financial commitment of homeownership.

Ultimately, the decision between an apartment and a house depends on individual circumstances, lifestyle preferences, and long-term financial goals. Both options have their own set of benefits and drawbacks, and the best choice varies from person to person.

Helpful Resources:

Check sites like www.airdna.co, www.usewheelhouse.com, www.beyondpricing.com or www.pricelabs.co. All of these sites are helpful when researching locations, pricing info and overall intel in the short-term rental space. The number one thing when looking for properties is safety. Make sure your properties are in a good friendly neighborhood to ensure your guests are safe. We will go into further detail during the online course.

Researching Locations

When looking for rental properties, thorough research is essential to ensure you find a place that fits your needs and budget. Here are the key steps and aspects to research:

1. Budgeting

- **Determine Affordability:** Calculate how much rent you can afford, typically no more than 30% of your monthly income.
- **Additional Costs:** Consider utilities, parking, renter's insurance, and other potential costs.

2. Location

- **Neighborhood:** Research the safety, amenities, and overall vibe of the neighborhood.
- **Commute:** Check the proximity to work, public transportation, schools, and essential services.
- **Future Development:** Look into any planned developments that might affect the area positively or negatively.

3. Lease Agreement

- **Terms and Conditions**: Understand the lease duration, renewal policies, and any penalties for breaking the lease.
- **Rent Increases**: Check for clauses related to rent increases and the frequency of such changes.
- **Subletting and Guests**: Know the rules regarding subletting and having guests stay for extended periods.

4. Amenities and Features

- **In-Unit Amenities**: Confirm the availability and condition of in-unit appliances, laundry facilities, heating/cooling systems, etc.

- **Building Amenities**: Evaluate the condition and availability of shared amenities like gyms, pools, common areas, etc.

5. Condition of the Property

- **Inspection**: Inspect the unit for any damages or issues before signing the lease.

- **Maintenance**: Ask about the process for requesting repairs and the average response time.

6. Tenant Rights and Local Laws

- **Local Regulations**: Familiarize yourself with tenant rights and local rental laws in your area.

- **Rent Control**: Check if the property is subject to rent control or stabilization laws.

7. Community and Environment

- **Noise Levels**: Visit the property at different times of the day to assess noise levels.

- **Neighbors**: Try to speak with current residents to get a sense of the community.

8. Security

- **Safety Measures**: Look for security features such as secure entrances, intercom systems, and surveillance cameras.

- **Crime Rates**: Research local crime rates and safety statistics for the area.

9. Utilities and Services

- **Included Utilities**: Know which utilities are included in the rent and which you'll need to pay separately.

- **Internet and Cable**: Check the availability and quality of internet and cable services in the building.

10. Pet Policies

- **Pet-Friendly**: If you have pets, ensure the property allows them and understand any associated fees or restrictions.

- **Nearby Pet Facilities**: Research nearby parks, veterinary services, and pet stores.

11. Parking and Transportation

- **Parking Availability**: Check if the property includes parking and any associated costs.

- **Public Transportation**: Evaluate the accessibility to public transportation options.

12. Utilities and Environmental Factors

- **Utility Costs**: Inquire about average utility costs from current or past tenants.

- **Environmental Factors**: Consider any environmental issues like flooding, noise pollution, or air quality.

By thoroughly researching these aspects, you can make an informed decision and find a rental property that meets your needs and preferences.

Platforms To List Your Property

- Airbnb www.airbnb.com
- VRBO www.vrbo.com
- Booking.com www.booking.com
- Expedia www.expedia.com
- Houses & Villas by Marriott International (HVM) www.homes-and-villas.marriott.com
- Homeaway www.homeaway.com
- TripAdvisor www.tripadvisor.com
- Website – Your own personal website www.yourwebsite.com

States That Are Viewed As Profitable

Profits from Airbnb or short-term rentals can vary significantly by state due to factors like tourism demand, local regulations, property values, and the cost of living. However, specific profit data by state is not always readily available due to the private nature of this information. Generally, profitability is higher in states with major tourist destinations or high urban density. Here are some states known for potentially high Airbnb profitability.

- **California**: Cities like Los Angeles, San Francisco, and San Diego are popular tourist destinations with high demand for short-term rentals.
- **Florida**: With cities like Miami, Orlando (home to Disney World), and beach destinations, Florida is a lucrative state for short-term rentals.
- **New York**: Particularly New York City, despite strict regulations, high demand can result in substantial profits.
- **Hawaii**: As a major tourist destination, short-term rentals in Hawaii, especially in Honolulu and Maui, can be highly profitable.
- **Texas**: Cities like Austin, known for its music festivals and tech scene, and Houston can offer profitable opportunities.
- **Nevada**: Las Vegas, with its constant influx of tourists, presents significant profit potential.
- **Colorado**: Cities like Denver and ski resort towns like Aspen and Vail are popular for both short-term and vacation rentals.
- **Tennessee**: Nashville, known for its music and cultural scene, is a profitable market for short-term rentals.
- **Arizona**: Cities like Phoenix and Scottsdale attract tourists year-round, especially during the winter months.
- **South Carolina**: Charleston and Myrtle Beach are popular tourist destinations with profitable short-term rental markets.

For a detailed and up-to-date analysis of Airbnb profits by state, consulting market research reports or data analytics platforms specializing in real estate and short-term rentals, such as AirDNA (www.airdna.co) or Mashvisor (www.mashvisor.com), can provide more specific insights.

Checklist

Kitchen
Kitchen Dish Towels and Rags
Pitcher
Plastic Utensils
Paper Plates
Plastic Cups
Napkins
Creamer/Half and Half
Sugar/Equal
Dishes (2 sets)
Pot and pans (2 sets)
Bowls
Glasses
Wine glasses
Utensils (metal)
Cooking utensils
Knife set
Dishwashing Liquid
Dishwasher Pods
Candy
Air Fryer
Keurig
Coffee Carousel
Kettle

Bedroom
Pillows
Sheet Sets (3-4 sets per bed)
Comforters (2 per bed)
Hangers

Essentials
Paper Towels
Tissue
Keypad – door entry

Outdoor Essentials
Grill Utensils
Grill

Bathroom
Blow Dryers (each room)
Hand soap
Bodywash
Shampoo/Conditioner
Towels

Cleaning Supplies
Bucket/Mop
Broom/Dustpan
Laundry Detergent/Bounce
Cleaning Products
Oven Cleaner (if needed)
Vacuum Cleaner

Creating A Budget/Profit Pivot

Months

Jan	
Feb	
Mar	
Apr	
May	
Jun	
Jul	
Aug	

Property

Belmont
Tyson

Category

ADT/Alarm
Airbnb
Booking
Electric
Gas
Internet
Mortgage/Rent
VRBO

Row Labels	Sum of Profit	Sum of Loss	Sum of Net Income
Jan	$ 9,971.50	$ 4,100.00	$ 5,871.50
Feb	$ 8,767.71	$ 5,474.00	$ 3,293.71
Mar	$ 22,167.14	$ 4,700.00	$ 17,467.14
Apr	$ 9,729.10	$ 4,700.00	$ 5,029.10
May	$ 6,654.20	$ 4,700.00	$ 1,954.20
Jun	$ 11,960.10	$ 4,700.00	$ 7,260.10
Jul	$ 7,502.67	$ 6,600.00	$ 902.67

Month			
Aug	$ 10,660.30	$ 6,600.00	$ 4,060.30
Sep	$	$ 6,600.00	$ (6,600.00)
Oct	$ 3,879.80	$ 6,600.00	$ (2,720.20)
Nov	$ 3,414.40	$ 6,600.00	$ (3,185.60)
Dec	$ 2,589.90	$ 6,600.00	$ (4,010.10)
Net	$ 97,296.82	$ 67,974.00	$ 29,322.82

Tracking Your Expenses

Begin Date	End Date	Days	Property	Category	Profit	Loss	Net Income
1/1/2023			Belmont		$ 9,971.50	$ -	$ 9,971.50
1/1/2023			Belmont	Mortgage/Rent		$ 4,100.00	$ (4,100.00)
1/1/2023			Tyson	Water		$ -	$ -
1/1/2023			Tyson	Gas		$ -	$ -
1/1/2023			Tyson	Electric		$ -	$ -
1/1/2023			Tyson	Internet		$ -	$ -
1/1/2023			Tyson	ADT/Alarm		$ -	$ -
1/1/2023			Belmont	Water		$ -	$ -
1/1/2023			Belmont	Gas		$ -	$ -
1/1/2023			Belmont	Electric		$ -	$ -
1/1/2023			Belmont	Internet		$ -	$ -
1/1/2023			Belmont	ADT/Alarm		$ -	$ -
2/1/2023			Tyson	Booking	$ 236.56	$ -	$ 236.56
2/1/2023			Tyson	Airbnb	$ 345.32	$ -	$ 345.32
2/1/2023			Tyson	VRBO	$ 270.63	$ -	$ 270.63

33

Date			Property	Category	Amount		
2/1/2023			Tyson	Mortgage/Rent		$ 1,374.00	$ (1,374.00)
2/1/2023			Belmont	Mortgage/Rent		$ 4,100.00	$ (4,100.00)
2/2/2023			Belmont	Airbnb	$ 1,891.50	$ -	$ 1,891.50
2/11/2023			Belmont	Airbnb	$ 4,258.30	$ -	$ 4,258.30
2/24/2023			Belmont	Airbnb	$ 1,765.40	$ -	$ 1,765.40
3/1/2023			Tyson	Mortgage/Rent		600.00	$ (600.00)
3/1/2023			Belmont	Mortgage/Rent		$ 4,100.00	$ (4,100.00)
3/3/2023			Belmont	Airbnb	$ 1,765.40	$ -	$ 1,765.40
3/10/2023			Belmont	Airbnb	$ 1,299.80	$ -	$ 1,299.80
3/11/2023			Tyson	Airbnb	$ 345.32	$ -	$ 345.32
3/17/2023			Tyson	Airbnb	$ 603.34	$ -	$ 603.34
3/17/2023			Belmont	Airbnb	$ 1,765.40	$ -	$ 1,765.40
3/20/2023	5/29/2023	70	Tyson	Airbnb	$ 13,303.28	$ -	$ 13,303.28
3/21/2023			Belmont	Airbnb	$ 1,319.20	$ -	$ 1,319.20
3/24/2023			Belmont	Airbnb	$ 1,765.40	$ -	$ 1,765.40
4/1/2023			Belmont	Airbnb	$ 1,891.50	$ -	$ 1,891.50
4/1/2023			Tyson	Mortgage/Rent		600.00	$ (600.00)

Date	Property	Category			
4/1/2023	Belmont	Mortgage/Rent		$ 4,100.00	$ (4,100.00)
4/5/2023	Belmont		$ 3,074.90	$ -	$ 3,074.90
4/14/2023	Belmont		$ 1,765.40	$ -	$ 1,765.40
4/21/2023	Belmont		$ 1,231.90	$ -	$ 1,231.90
4/28/2023	Belmont		$ 1,765.40	$ -	$ 1,765.40
5/1/2023	Tyson	Mortgage/Rent		600.00	$ (600.00)
5/1/2023	Belmont	Mortgage/Rent		4,100.00	$ (4,100.00)
5/4/2023	Belmont	Airbnb	$ 1,765.40	$ -	$ 1,765.40
5/11/2023	Belmont	Airbnb	$ 1,823.60	$ -	$ 1,823.60
5/19/2023	Belmont	Airbnb	$ 1,765.40	$ -	$ 1,765.40
5/27/2023	Belmont	Airbnb	$ 1,299.80	$ -	$ 1,299.80
6/1/2023	Belmont	Airbnb	$ 3,414.40	$ -	$ 3,414.40
6/1/2023	Tyson	Mortgage/Rent		600.00	$ (600.00)
6/1/2023	Belmont	Mortgage/Rent		4,100.00	$ (4,100.00)
6/9/2023	Belmont	Airbnb	$ 1,823.60	$ -	$ 1,823.60
6/16/2023	Belmont	Airbnb	$ 2,483.20	$ -	$ 2,483.20
6/22/2023	Belmont	Airbnb	$ 1,823.60	$ -	$ 1,823.60

Date	Property	Type	Income	Expense	Net
6/29/2023	Belmont	Airbnb	$ 2,415.30	$ -	$ 2,415.30
7/1/2023	Tyson	Mortgage/Rent		$ 2,500.00	$ (2,500.00)
7/1/2023	Belmont	Mortgage/Rent		$ 4,100.00	$ (4,100.00)
7/13/2023	Tyson	Airbnb	$ 1,338.60	$ -	$ 1,338.60
7/13/2023	Belmont	Airbnb	$ 2,589.90	$ -	$ 2,589.90
7/13/2023	Belmont	Airbnb	$ 1,338.60	$ -	$ 1,338.60
7/21/2023	Tyson	VRBO	$ 518.67	$ -	$ 518.67
7/28/2023	Belmont	Airbnb	$ 1,299.80	$ -	$ 1,299.80
7/29/2023	Tyson	Airbnb	$ 417.10	$ -	$ 417.10
8/1/2023	Tyson	Mortgage/Rent		$ 2,500.00	$ (2,500.00)
8/1/2023	Belmont	Mortgage/Rent		$ 4,100.00	$ (4,100.00)
8/5/2023	Belmont	Airbnb	$ 3,007.00	$ -	$ 3,007.00
8/11/2023	Belmont	Airbnb	$ 2,589.90	$ -	$ 2,589.90
8/30/2023	Belmont	Airbnb	$ 5,063.40	$ -	$ 5,063.40
9/1/2023	Tyson	Mortgage/Rent		$ 2,500.00	$ (2,500.00)
9/1/2023	Belmont	Mortgage/Rent		$ 4,100.00	$ (4,100.00)
10/1/2023	Tyson	Mortgage/Rent		$ 2,500.00	$ (2,500.00)

Date	Property	Type	Income	Expense	Net
10/1/2023	Belmont	Mortgage/Rent		$ 4,100.00	$ (4,100.00)
10/6/2023	Belmont	Airbnb	$ 2,589.90	$ -	$ 2,589.90
10/20/2023	Belmont	Airbnb	$ 1,289.90	$ -	$ 1,289.90
11/2/2023	Tyson	Mortgage/Rent		2,500.00	$ (2,500.00)
11/2/2023	Belmont	Mortgage/Rent		$ 4,100.00	$ (4,100.00)
11/22/2023	Belmont	Airbnb	3,414.40	$ -	$ 3,414.40
12/1/2023	Tyson	Mortgage/Rent		2,500.00	$ (2,500.00)
12/1/2023	Belmont	Mortgage/Rent		4,100.00	$ (4,100.00)
12/14/2023	Belmont	Airbnb	$ 2,589.90	$ -	2,589.90

Furnishing The Property

Furnish your properties with your unique style, but ensure you prioritize quality when selecting furniture.

Here are a few things to consider:

1. Design and Architecture

- **Unique Architecture**: Distinctive architectural features or historical significance.
- **Interior Design**: Thoughtfully designed interiors that reflect a unique style or theme.

2. Amenities

- **Smart Home Features**: Integration of smart home technology for added convenience and security.

3. Space and Layout

- **Open Floor Plans**: Spacious and flexible living areas.
- **Custom Layouts**: Unique floor plans that cater to various lifestyle needs.

4. Furnishings

- **Quality Furniture**: High-quality, stylish furnishings that enhance comfort and aesthetic appeal.
- **Personal Touch**: Decor and furniture that reflect your personal taste and style.

5. Sustainability

- **Eco-Friendly Features**: Energy-efficient appliances, solar panels, and sustainable building materials.

6. Outdoor Spaces

- **Private Outdoor Areas**: Balconies, patios, or gardens that offer private outdoor living.

7. History and Character

- **Historical Charm**: Properties with a rich history or unique story.
- **Character Details**: Original features like hardwood floors, exposed brick, or vintage fixtures.

8. Safety and Security

- **Advanced Security**: Enhanced security systems and safe neighborhood.
- **Privacy**: Well-designed layouts that offer privacy from neighbors.

9. Flexibility

- **Versatility**: Spaces that can be adapted for various uses, such as home offices, guest rooms, or hobby areas.

By highlighting these aspects, you can showcase what makes your property stand out and appeal to potential renters.

Finding Reliable Cleaners

Cleaners, Cleaners, Cleaners

Cleaners either make or break your business. It is very important to ensure you hire the right cleaners that will not only meet your needs but meet the needs of your customers/guests. Try out several cleaners until you find the right one.

- Make a checklist of what is important for your cleaners to abide by (see sample).
- Provide feedback to your cleaners regularly so they are always learning and growing. If you find anything out of place, be sure to let them know so you keep the lines of communication open.
- Find cleaners that are reasonably priced. You can certainly pass this fee onto your guests, but you want to make sure it's fair. You don't want customers to pass up on your property due to cleaning fees.

Cleaners Checklist

Additional Task
Walk the house - check for damages; cut off the games at Belmont, 125 Cedar, Bluff and Spring Rock
Wash Linen
Make up beds
Paper Towels in each bathroom
Tissue in each bathroom
Two rolls of tissue under each sink
Hand Soap in each bathroom (as needed)
Hand Towels in sinks
Check under beds for trash/other items
Check under couches for trash/other items
Refill each basket in the rooms with towels
Start dishwasher or wash dishes
Replenish the coffee pods (Carousel)
Replenish creamer
Throw out used coffee pods in the Keurig (when applicable)
Check the oven - if it needs to be cleaned, turn on self-cleaner (once a month)
Replenish pantry - paper plates, napkins, cutlery, and two rolls of paper towels
Empty trash can in garage
Wipe tables off in the garage
Wipe table outside enclosed porch (Belmont)
Replenish candy in candy jars
Check Air fryer - clean

Finding A Good Integrator

Here is a list of integrators that are helpful when automating your Airbnb or short-term rental business. It is important to partner up with one of these organizations to keep your business running smoothly and to avoid a lot of mishaps. Some of these organizations have the ability to help you build your own website or link to your current website to start receiving private bookings. We will go over these in grave detail during the online course.

www.hostaway.com

www.hospitable.com

www.rentmanager.com

www.igms.com

www.guesty.com

www.lodgify.com

Identifying Property Management Personnel

Identifying the right property management personnel is crucial for the smooth operation and maintenance of your property. Here are key qualities and steps to help you find the right candidates:

Key Qualities of Property Management Personnel

1. Experience and Expertise

- **Industry Knowledge:** Understanding of property management laws, tenant rights, and market trends.
- **Previous Experience:** Proven track record in managing similar properties.

2. Communication Skills

- **Clear Communication:** Ability to effectively communicate with property owners, tenants, and vendors.
- **Problem-Solving:** Skilled in resolving conflicts and addressing tenant concerns promptly.

3. Organizational Skills

- **Detail-Oriented:** Meticulous in handling paperwork, leases, and financial records.
- **Time Management:** Ability to prioritize tasks and manage multiple responsibilities efficiently.

4. Technical Skills

- **Tech-Savvy:** Proficiency in using property management software and other relevant technologies.
- **Maintenance Knowledge:** Understanding of basic property maintenance and repair procedures.

5. Customer Service Orientation

- o **Tenant Relations: Focused on providing excellent customer service to ensure tenant satisfaction.**

- o **Professionalism: Polite, respectful, and professional demeanor.**

6. Flexibility and Availability

- o **Responsive: Available to handle emergencies and urgent situations.**

- o **Adaptable: Willing to adapt to changing circumstances and property needs.**

Customer Service Plan

Your number one goal should be to provide exceptional customer service, enhance guest satisfaction, and build a strong reputation. I cannot stress enough how important customer service goes along way when dealing with your customers/guests. I have seen so many hosts get into this business and due to several customer service mishaps, their ratings go down the drain. Once your ratings take a hit, it is hard to come back from. Not saying you can't recover but it is harder than just having a great customer service plan upfront. Your plan should include how quickly you plan to respond to guests or upcoming guests when they reach out. Do you have the proper people in place should an issue or emergency arise? What will set you apart? What are some things you can do inside of the property to ensure a great customer experience? There are so many more things when it comes to customer service. See below for an outline of a customer service plan. A good customer service plan in the hospitality industry focuses on providing exceptional guest experiences, fostering customer loyalty, and encouraging positive word-of-mouth referrals. Here's a comprehensive plan:

Staff Training and Development

- **Comprehensive Training:** Ensure all staff receive training in customer service, including communication skills, problem-solving, and cultural sensitivity.
- **Ongoing Development:** Provide regular training updates and professional development opportunities to keep skills current.

2. Customer Interaction

- **Warm Welcome:** Greet guests with a friendly and professional attitude.

- **Personalization:** Use guest names and remember their preferences to create a personalized experience.
- **Effective Communication:** Listen actively to guests' needs and respond promptly.

3. Quality Assurance

- **Consistent Standards:** Establish and maintain high standards for cleanliness, safety, and service quality.
- **Feedback Mechanisms:** Implement systems for guests to provide feedback, such as comment cards, surveys, or digital platforms.
- **Regular Audits:** Conduct regular audits to maintain the highest standards and identify areas for improvement.

4. Problem Resolution

- **Empower Staff:** Enable employees to resolve issues on the spot without needing managerial approval.
- **Swift Response:** Address complaints and issues immediately to prevent escalation.
- **Follow-Up:** Follow-up communication is important to ensure that the problem has been resolved to the guest's satisfaction.

5. Technology Integration

- **Reservation Systems:** Use advanced reservation and check-in systems to streamline processes and reduce wait times.
- **Communication Tools:** Implement tools like chatbots, mobile apps, and social media to enhance communication with guests.
- **Customer Relationship Management (CRM):** Utilize CRM systems to track guest preferences and history for a more personalized service.

6. Amenities and Extras

- **Value-Added Services:** Offer complimentary services such as Wi-Fi, breakfast, or shuttle services.
- **Special Requests:** Accommodate special requests and provide unexpected delights (e.g., complimentary upgrades or surprise treats).

7. Employee Satisfaction

- **Positive Work Environment:** Foster a supportive and positive work environment to keep employees motivated and engaged.
- **Recognition and Rewards:** Recognize and reward outstanding performance and customer service excellence.

8. Community and Sustainability

- **Local Engagement:** Engage with the local community through partnerships, events, and promotions.
- **Sustainable Practices:** Implement environmentally friendly practices to appeal to eco-conscious guests and reduce operational costs.

9. Marketing and Promotion

- **Social Proof:** Encourage satisfied guests to leave positive reviews on platforms like TripAdvisor, Yelp, and Google.
- **Loyalty Programs:** Develop loyalty programs to reward repeat guests and incentivize return visits.
- **Targeted Marketing:** Use data analytics to create targeted marketing campaigns that appeal to specific guest segments.

10. Continuous Improvement

- **Analyze Feedback:** Regularly analyze guest feedback and service performance metrics to identify trends and areas for improvement.
- **Innovate:** Stay updated with industry trends and continuously innovate to enhance the guest experience.

Questions/Answers/Notes

Congratulations – you made it to the end! Your final piece of homework is to write a letter congratulating yourself on your first year in business. Write this letter in great detail outlining where you see yourself in a year. Give lots of detail!

Notes:

You made it! 😊

www.ingramcontent.com/pod-product-compliance
Lightning Source LLC
Chambersburg PA
CBHW081748200326
41597CB00024B/4436